JUST YOUR LUCK

Where to find
sweepstakes, games,
and instant wins, online,
with $1000's in cash
and prizes to give away…
all for *free!*

Wayne Brown

River Street
Publishing

Just Your Luck
Contents

Chapter 3 Sweepstakes/Contests Blogs

Chapter 4 Instant Win

Chapter 5 Online Games

Introduction

Real people actually win! I know I was a little skeptical of the online promotions, sweepstakes, instant wins, and games promising money and prizes. Could these companies really give away all of this cash and merchandise? Could HGTV really give away a Dream Home? Can a person play free games online and win $25, $50, and even $1000's of dollars? The answer is yes. A check for $10,000 from Lycos Gamesville made me a believer.

Sure, the odds are out of this world, sometimes, with hundreds, thousands, and even millions of entries for certain sweepstakes, but somebody's going to win. It might as well be you! With the advent of the computer, companies found a relatively inexpensive way to reach out to millions of people. Online sweepstakes, instant wins, and games provided a win-win for business and consumers. In exchange for viewing a company's newest product or promotion, an individual gets a chance to win money and prizes ranging from a $1.00 coupon to a new Mustang to a vacation of a lifetime to a new dream home.

In Just Your Luck, we've organized these opportunities into categories including sweepstakes sites, sites with sweeps, sweepstakes blogs, instant wins, and online games. (All Free!) We've then provided a description of each site, pros, cons, ratings, and comments.

Look through the listings. There's sure to be something that interests you, whether it's entering sweeps, playing games, or trying an instant win. Just be sure to read the rules, check whether you wish to receive e-mails, (most sites have a box for this) and remember your passwords if you have to join a site. You won't regret it if you write them down and keep them near. In fact, we've included some pages at the back of this book for passwords.

We've made every effort to accurately describe the sites listed in this book, but over time, companies and websites may change or evolve. Again, read the rules, do your own research if needed. Also, support the companies who provide you these opportunities. If their promotions are successful, chances are they'll do more of them in the future.

Finally, remember, you might not win anything right away, perhaps you'll never win a huge prize, but chances are you'll have fun. Of course, there's always that chance, you'll hit it big. So why are you waiting?

Good luck!

Chapter 1 Sweepstakes Sites

Chapter 1 Sweepstakes Sites

Site: About.com Contests & Sweepstakes http://contests.about.com

Membership: No

Site Design/Navigation: Pleasing bright look, sweeps start on home page.

Description: Maintained by Sandra Grauschopf, an About.com guide, the site has been redesigned since we first visited. With lots of sweeps, clicking on one will give you a go between page with links to sweepstakes' entry page or rules. Sweeps were good and up to date on our last visit. In addition, there were some interesting articles to read on the home page.

Pros: Personal touch, good variety of sweeps.

Cons: If you decide to enter sweepstakes, you'll have to go back to the go between page, and then back one more time to return to the About website.

Our Rating: ✪✪✪✪

Comments: Good graphic redesign, good sweeps, and good articles.

Chapter 1 Sweepstakes Sites

Site: UltraContest http://www.ultracontest.com

Membership: No, but free membership entitles you to set favorites and access entry tracker.

Site Design/Navigation: Colorful, very organized, info loaded pages give this website an advantage over some other sites. No need to go looking for details on sweeps, it seems that most information is included.

Description: Loads of information on sweepstakes, tons of high quality sweeps, and easy entry make the Ultra Contest website a must to try out. Tabs at top list prize categories as well as daily entries and favorites. When we last visited, we found it difficult to stop entering sweepstakes, since there were so many good ones listed. A winner's circle button can also be found at the top of the home page.

Pros: Number of great sweepstakes, easy entry.

Cons: No expiring soon category.

Our Rating: ✪✪✪✪ 1/2

Comments: You will not find many smaller sweeps here.

Chapter 1 Sweepstakes Sites

Site: Last Chance Sweepstakes www.lastchancesweepstakes.com

Membership: No, but you can sign up for free newsletter.

Site Design/Navigation: Simple, with one column of sweepstakes.

Description: Last Chance Sweepstakes lists only sweepstakes that are about to expire. When we last visited, there were seven pages of sweeps that would expire in two days. Sweeps included both big and small giveaways, from books to a Disney Caribbean cruise vacation. The site is easy to navigate, since there is only one category of sweeps. In fact, there are no other categories at all.

Pros: Good list of expiring sweepstakes.

Cons: No other tabs or categories.

Our Rating: ✪✪✪✪1/2

Comments: Last Chance Sweepstakes does one thing, and does a a pretty good job of it. If you're looking for other categories of sweeps, you'll have to look elsewhere.

Chapter 1 Sweepstakes Sites

Site: Arlana's Corner www.arlanascorner.com

Membership: No

Site Design/Navigation: Compact home page with links in middle, and a drop down menu.

Description: Arlana's Corner has links for twenty categories, including sweeps, games, other sweeps' sites, freebies, etc. The drop down menu has some other links listed. The sweepstakes section is organized by one entry, daily, weekly, monthly, and instant wins. When we last checked, there were as many as twenty three sweeps in a certain category but many were outdated.

Pros: Free, lots of categories, you might find something different here.

Cons: Daily entry category dominated by Consumer Expressions and Winning Surveys/Sweeps, lots of outdated sweeps.

Our Rating: ✪ ½

Comments: We like all the different categories. Real good major sweeps are limited in number, though, and we're disappointed that many of the sweepstakes were outdated. We'll check back.

Chapter 1 Sweepstakes Sites

Site: Contest Listing www.contestlisting.com

Membership: No

Site Design/Navigation: Colorful page full of images of prizes being given away. Three tabs at top left include prize categories, entry method, and country.

Description: Contest Listing describes itself as a site to promote company giveaways. A click on any of the prize images will bring up an informational page with a link to the giveaway. When we first visited, we were not sure of the promotions, to be honest. However, after looking around, we found some interesting giveaways. In fact, there were eleven pages with prizes from pet items to new cars.

Pros: A different type of site with a wide variety of promotions.

Cons: The giveaway's sponsor is not always listed on the first page.

Our Rating: ✪✪✪

Comments: The Contest Listing site is not your typical sweepstakes' site. When we last visited, we found links to companies and sites that we'll visit in the future.

Chapter 1 Sweepstakes Sites

Site: Contest Chest http://contestchest.com/

Membership: Yes

Site Design/Navigation: Very easy navigation with few categories.

Description: After visiting the home page, and selecting your country, you get a list of giveaways. When you register, you can also narrow the sweeps to your preferences. When we first visited, there were over twenty six hundred available to enter. A tab at the top right allows you to sort by expiration date, with the sweeps varied from gift cards to trips.

Pros: A good variety of sweeps, simple navigation.

Cons: Lack of categories, giveaway sponsor not listed on first page.

Our Rating: ✪✪✪

Comments: Contest Chest might be a good site to visit to see if the format appeals to you.

Chapter 1 Sweepstakes Sites

Site: Infinite Sweeps www.infinitesweeps.com

Membership: Not required, but free membership entitles you to several special features including e-mail updates, last entry time, and the ability to save favorites.

Site Design/Navigation: Easy to navigate once you get familiar with the site. Tabs at top and bottom, and categories on on the right side of the home page give you a lot of information to look over.

Description: Infinite Sweeps has lots of categories including latest sweeps, sweepstakes ending today, tomorrow, this week, this month, types of entry, prizes, entry frequency, and more. On our last visit, we entered giveaways without finding any expired dates. In fact, there were as many sweeps for cars and cash that we remember a site listing. These sweeps included entries for well-known brands like Ford, but also some that might not be so familiar to most people.

Pros: Number of sweepstakes, and lots of information.

Cons: Might take too much of your time.

Our Rating: ✪✪✪✪✪

Comments: Infinite Sweeps might require multiple visits to take in all that the site offers you.

Chapter 1 Sweepstakes Sites

Site: Sweepon www.sweepon.com

Membership: No

Site Design/Navigation: Colorful, loaded with images, easy to navigate.

Description: Sweepon is an advertiser supported site of selected sweeps and instant wins. When we visited, the site had eleven pages of giveaways featuring prizes from cleaning products to a million dollar prize. Giveaways are presented as boxes of images, representing prizes being given away. You are given a description of the giveaway, and then you must watch a video to complete your entry.

Pros: Colorful, easy to follow site.

Cons: Only prize categories, sweepstakes sponsor not always listed on the first page.

Our Rating: ✪✪✪

Comments: A different kind of sweepstakes site that you might like.

Chapter 1 Sweepstakes Sites

Site: Sweepstakes Today http://www.sweepstakestoday.com

Membership: Yes

Site Design/Navigation: Clean looking site, easy to find links.

Description: Sweepstakes Today's home page, when we last visited, read that the site had 800+ sweepstakes listed, totaling over $81 million in cash and prizes. We did not count, but the site has lots of sweeps, along with a variety of categories and links. At the top of the home page, links include hot, featured, new, prizes,and winner's list. You'll find sweeps and prize categories at the bottom.

Pros: Number of sweeps, variety, and good descriptions.

Cons: Sweepstakes don't open in a new page.

Our Rating: ✪✪✪✪ ½

Comments: When you click on a sweep, you get a page with a good look at the giveaway, with links, rating, details, and more.

Chapter 1 Sweepstakes Sites

Site: AllTop Contests http://contests.alltop.com

Membership: No

Site Design/Navigation: Good, easy to read, well organized.

Description: AllTop Contests' home page features twenty plus sites with headlnes of the latest posts or articles. All of these headlines are links to the respective sites. The sites range from 99 Designs to Enter Online Sweeps to Sweepstakes Mania.One nice feature is the ability to see more info when you hover over a post.

Pros: Lots of sites, headlines, links open in a new page.

Cons: Contests, sweeps, competitions all mixed together

Our Rating: ✪✪✪✪

Comments: We like that the site is different from other sites.

Chapter 1 Sweepstakes Sites

Site: Online-Sweepstakes www.online-sweepstakes.com

Membership: No, but registration required for extra features such as My Sweeps, and to post on forums.

Site Design/Navigation: Very good, easy to read, categories prominent on home page.

Description: Online-Sweepstakes has one of the easiest to read home pages packed with categories and information, including new sweepstakes, an expiring soon category, sweeps by entry frequency, prizes, sweepstakes resources, and types of sweeps and contests. Number of sweeps, contests, etc. listed by category on home page.

Pros: Lists of different categories with numbers, message boards, easy to navigate, expires soon category.

Cons: Smaller type, many sweeps with smaller prizes, however, some may like these sweeps with greater odds.

Our Rating: ✪✪✪✪ ½

Comments: Site is well organized with good variety of sweeps, info, and a good message board. A variety of links including instant wins and contests is also included.

Chapter 1 Sweepstakes Sites

Site: Any Lucky Day www.anyluckyday.com

Membership: No, but e-mail required for daily e-mail.

Site Design/Navigation: No categories, just boxes with giveaways.

Description: The site has changed from when we first visited. Now, Any Lucky Day has just one page of giveaways from various companies, with prizes ranging from gift cards to merchandise to trips. While we found some nice sweepstakes on our last visit, we also noticed that there were some expired giveaways on the home page.

Pros: Easy to look through sweepstakes.

Cons: First look doesn't always reveal sponsor or details.

Our Rating: ✪✪

Comments: If you like categories, you'll have to look elsewhere.

Chapter 1 Sweepstakes Sites

Site: Contest Queen www.contestqueen.com

Membership: No

Site Design/Navigation: Simple, graphic, easy to find links.

Description: The Contest Queen website, which is run by Carolyn Wilman, from Canada, has a wealth of information and resources on contests/sweeps. The site is not a directory of links to sweeps but rather a site that deals with most anything to do with giveaways. Links include sweepstakes' clubs, conventions, sweepstakes' sites, suppliers, and more.

Pros: Information, links, inspiration.

Cons: No list of current sweepstakes.

Our Rating: ✪✪✪✪✪

Comments: The Contest Queen website is a good resource for the person interested in sweepstakes, and a good place for inspiration.

Chapter 1 Sweepstakes Sites

Site: 1 Sweepstakes http://1sweepstakes.com

Membership: No, but e-mail address required for free newsletter.

Site Design/Navigation: Fairly simple, straightforward design with latest sweeps listed directly on home page, categories and blogroll on left.

Description: 1 Sweepstakes offers a number of both large and small sweeps. No category is available for sweeps ending soon. An archives listing, on left, actually goes back to 2007, But not sure when you would actually need that.

Pros: You might find some good sweeps in the mix.

Cons: Prize categories contain too many older sweeps.

Our Rating: ✪✪✪

Comments: You might find a good giveaway here, recent comments section seems to have no connection with sweeps.

Chapter 1 Sweepstakes Sites

Site: Giveaway Frenzy http://giveawayfrenzy.com

Membership: No

Site Design/Navigation: Not too difficult to figure out. The latest and featured giveaways fill up the home page, with categories at top left.

Description: Giveaway Frenzy has an assortment of giveaways listed, along with prize categories and instant wins. The sweeps seem to be an even mix of giveaways with smaller prizes and bigger prizes. On our last visit, we found sweeps for $25.00 gift cards and also $30,000 trucks. In fact, there is a category that lists sweeps by value of cash prize. Most sweepstakes are entered by simply clicking on entry page. However, Giveaway Frenzy requires that you click on a share, like, or tweet button for direct entry link to some sweeps listed on their site.

Pros: Nice assortment of giveaways.

Cons: Some giveaways require additional click.

Our Rating: ✪✪✪ 1/2

Comments: Interesting assortment of sweeps that you might like.

Chapter 1 Sweepstakes Sites

Site: Contest Girl www.contestgirl.com

Membership: No, but e-mail address required to access the My Contests feature or to subscribe to the free newsletter.

Site Design/Navigation: Well organized, info presented clearly, but at first glance, you might not think the site would have as many good sweepstakes.

Description: When we first visited, we immediately liked the personal feel. The site states, "Welcome to my sweepstakes website, I'm Linda. Today is--, I have – active contests listed, -- today." Latest numbers on our last visit were 4,320 active sweeps, 132 new sweeps. In the center of the home page, you'll find a winner's list. On the left, you'll find sweeps listed by U.S. or Canadian, single entry, daily, weekly, monthly, and odd entry. Other information and links include contest tips, faq, What I've Won, contest archives, and more.

Pros: Lots of sweeps, info presented clearly.

Cons: Ads between sweeps, if we have to find one, but most are geared toward sweeps.

Our Rating: ✪✪✪✪ ½

Comments: If you rollover the sorted by posted date tab, you get a drop down menu of other ways to sort sweeps.

Chapter 1 Sweepstakes Sites

Site: Sweepstakes Lovers www.sweepstakeslovers.com

Membership: No, but e-mail address required for free newsletter.

Site Design/Navigation: Lots going on here..graphics, info…might take a little while to sort out.

Description: Recently added sweepstakes are listed on home page with featured sweeps at top. Up at the top, you'll find categories with entry frequency. At the bottom, you'll also find those categories, along with prize categories. When you click on a sweep, you'll get a page with lots of info including a link to the giveaway.

Pros: Some good sweeps, lots of info.

Cons: No ending soon category; after entering sweep, you'll have to hit back button to get back to sweepstakes list.

Our Rating: ✪✪✪

Comments: Lots of good sweeps when we last visited.

Chapter 1 Sweepstakes Sites

Site: Sweepstakes Max http://sweepstakesmax.com

Membership: No, but free membership entitles you to several features.

Site Design/Navigation: Simple to navigate, easy to read.

Description: Sweepstakes Max has one of the easiest formats to find and enter sweeps. The giveaways are immediately presented to you on the home page. If you want to filter or sort them, the drop down lists are located at top. When we last visited, we had more than enough listings to keep us busy, even when sorting them by those sweeps ending first. A good mixture of smaller and larger sweepstakes can be found including those with blockbuster prizes such as cars, trips, and cash. A good feature is the fact that the sweeps open in a new window, making it easy to get back to the list of sweeps.

Pros: Number of sweeps, and they open in a new window.

Cons: Sponsor of sweeps is not always listed on first page.

Our Rating: ✪✪✪✪✪

Comments: We'll check back to see if Sweepstakes Max can keep up with the number of sweeps, and the ease of use.

Chapter 1 Sweepstakes Sites

Site: Sweepstakes Bible www.sweepstakesbible.com

Membership: No, but members can use My Sweepstakes feature to track sweeps that they enter.

Site Design/Navigation: Simple, no frills site with only home page, latest entries, and expiring soon categories.

Description: Sweepstakes Bible, while it lists some very good sweeps, does not have the features of some other sites. When we last visited, we found sweeps from such names as Shoe Carnival, HGTV, Hot Topic, Nissan, and Applebees. The prizes ranged from back to school merchandise to the HGTV Urban Oasis valued at over $500,000. The sweeps are listed with some info on the first page, but listings don't include whether the entry has any requirements.

Pros: Simple, colorful, easy to read design, up to date sweeps.

Cons: Sweeps don't open in a new window, only three categories.

Our Rating: ✪✪✪1/2

Comments: We've found some nice sweeps on Sweepstakes Bible, but more categories would definitely be a plus.

Chapter 1 Sweepstakes Sites

Site: Win Prizes Online www.winprizesonline.com

Membership: No, but free membership entitles you to entry tracking, save favorites, participate in forum, and winner's list.

Site Design/Navigation: Win Prizes Online has a number of options to sort through sweeps, which is good. However, the home page is very busy, and you'll have to learn to find your way around first.

Description: While Win Prizes Online features some good sweepstakes, entering them can be more than a one step process, at least if you're not a member. Once you find the enter sweeps tab, you'll face a membership reminder every time you try to enter a giveaway. Sure, it's just another click, but it can be a little annoying. On the other hand, the site offers a wide range of sweeps and multiple ways to sort through them.

Pros: Sorting options, features with free membership.

Cons: Lots of ads, more than one step to enter sweeps.

Our Rating: ✪✪✪

Comments: Busy pages, but the site does offer some good sweeps.

Chapter 1 Sweepstakes Sites

Site: Sweepstakes Daily www.sweepstakesdaily.com

Membership: No, but you can subscribe to get new sweeps in e-mail.

Site Design/Navigation: Minimal, but colorful design. With one row of tabs at top, navigation is easy.

Description: When we last visited, Sweepstakes Daily listed quite a few outstanding sweeps for cars, trips, and cash, but also some for smaller prizes. The prizes, frequency, and expires tabs had a number of categories. We always like sweeps that are organized by expiration date, so the expires tab fits the bill. While the sweepstakes entry page opens in a new window, you must first go to sweeps info page, which does not open in a new window. Lots of info on giveaway, but this does involve one more step.

Pros: Tab categories, clean look of site, good sweeps.

Cons: Two-step process to enter sweepstakes.

Our Rating: ✪✪✪ 1/2

Comments: On our last visit, the sweepstakes were good and plentiful.

Chapter 1 Sweepstakes Sites

Site: Best Sweepstakes www.bestsweepstakes.com

Membership: No, unless you subscribe to their newsletters.

Site Design/Navigation: Very simple, once you get familiar with the site. The newest sweeps are located on the right side under the header. Click Online Sweepstakes tab under Sweepstakes Forum to get full list of all giveaways.

Description: At first glance, Best Sweepstakes appears to be just an ad for their newsletters, but there are lots of good sweepstakes listed here. The newest sweeps and full list of sweeps list a good deal of info up front, including expiration dates. The info also lets you know the number of entries allowed, and prize given away. Best of all, the sweeps all open in a new window. When we last visited, we found giveaways for trips all around the world, cash, and cars.

Pros: Easy sweepstakes entry, sweeps open in a new window.

Cons: Not quite as many sweeps as some other sites.

Our Rating: ✪✪✪✪

Comments: Some good sweepstakes are available. Click Online Sweeps link under Sweepstakes Forum to access categories.

Chapter 1 Sweepstakes Sites

Site: Sweepstakes Advantage www.sweepsadvantage.com

Membership: Not required, but membership lets you take advantage of special features including forums, access to expiring soon category, and members' giveaways.

Site Design/Navigation: For the non-member, you have to take some time to get familiar with the tabs you are allowed to use, and those that you cannot access. Once you go through this learning process, the site is easy to navigate.

Description: If you don't care to join, you can access the new sweepstakes, as well as the popular sweeps categories located on the home page. The expiring soon category is reserved for members. On our last visit, we found lots of good sweeps from companies such as Walmart, Coke, hhgregg, and Saks Fifth Avenue. We also found sweeps from such sites as Win Loot and Cash Dazzle which you may or may not like so much. However, the listing of sweeps is extensive.

Pros*:* Lots of good sweepstakes, sweeps open in new window.

Cons: No access to certain categories unless you're a member.

Our Rating: ✪✪✪

Comments: You could find some good sweeps here. You can also learn some info on sweepstakes rules and laws.

Chapter 1 Sweepstakes Sites

Site: Big Sweeps www.bigsweeps.com

Membership: Not required for some sweeps, required for most.

Site Design/Navigation: No sweeps on home page. You must click tabs for sweeps. If you're not a member, though, you won't have too much to access.

Description: Big Sweeps is designed more for the premium user, it seems. When we tried to access sweeps on our first visit, we found mostly sweeps that were limited to paid subscribers. After signing up for the free membership, we were still limited in the number of giveaways that we could access. The sweeps also were limited to the smaller variety, with prizes of gift cards, books, baskets, and smaller cash awards. There were some sweeps with larger prizes, but most of those could only be accessed by premium users.

Pros: Lots of sweeps with smaller prizes and greater odds of winning.

Cons: Limited number of sweeps available to free users, small type.

Our Rating: ✪✪

Comments: Click on the instant win tabs, then click on categories with different prizes, to access more sweepstakes.

Chapter 1 Sweepstakes Sites

Site: Hypersweep www.hypersweep.com

Membership: Not required for basic sweeps. Paid membership gets users special features.

Site Design/Navigation: Home page has four sections with links to info, sweeps, forums, and adding sweeps. Click on Open the Basic Sweepbot to get sweeps' listings.

Description: While the Hypersweep home page is not too impressive, a click to see the sweepstakes' listing might give you a little different feeling. The Sweepbot, which you will access, is basically a search tool for sweeps. When we used it on our last visit, we were impressed by the number of sweeps that were available, especially those with larger prizes. Our first search revealed giveaways for $100,000, $200,000, cars, trips, and merchandise from well-known companies.

Pros: Sweeps presented in a simple, easy to read list, number of good sweepstakes available.

Cons: Could not figure out how to use computer's autofill feature with Hypersweep's basic sweepbot.

Our Rating: ✪✪✪✪✪

Comments: Great list of sweeps with nice prizes.

Chapter 2 Sites with Sweeps

.

Chapter 2 Sites with Sweeps

Site: Nascar www.nascar.com

Membership: Required to enter contests/sweeps.

Contests/Sweeps Section: No

Description: Good selection of contests/sweeps first time we visited, with five contests/sweeps featured, including the American Ethanol Sweepstakes, with the chance to win 1 of 3 Chevy Silverados. Two fantasy games and one promotion from Quicken Loans were available on our second and third visits. Our next visit found a chance to visit Las Vegas for Nascar Champion's Week, and participate in all kinds of events. We were disappointed on our most recent visit. Only one giveaway was listed, that being found on a Honda advertisement. Also there was no longer a section with sweepstakes.

Our Rating: ✪

Comments: Good site for racing fans, we'll check back to see if more giveaways are listed.

Chapter 2 Sites with Sweeps

Site: The Celebrity Café www.thecelebritycafe.com

Membership: No

Contests/Sweeps Section: Yes. Contests tab at top right.

Description: Our first visit to The Celebrity Café found contests/sweeps with prizes ranging from a trip to San Francisco to a $1000 gift certificate, from Moon River pearls to a $100 spa package to a set of sixty compact discs. What a selection! The next time we checked the site, we found thirty contests/sweeps. Prizes ranged from dvd's, prize packs, to ipods, PSP's, guitars, and more. Our most recent visit found seven contests/sweeps with most of the prizes being of the smaller variety.

Our Rating: ✪✪✪✪

Comments: The Celebrity Café is quite an assortment of info about cd's, celebrities, movies, books, and more. It's worth a visit to check out the site and all of the giveaways.

Chapter 2 Sites with Sweeps

Site: Visit South http://visitsouth.com/contests/

Membership: No

Contests/Sweeps Section: Yes. Contests and Deals tab at top right.

Description: Visit South, a production of Compass Media, promotes tourism in the southern United States. The giveaways that the site offers, features getaways to spots in the region. On our last visit, there were five trips available to win, with stays on the Alabama gulf coast, and the North Carolina outer banks available to win.

Our Rating: ✪✪1/2

Comments: The prizes are nice, not huge, but the odds of winning are a little better, no doubt, than major sweepstakes.

Chapter 2 Sites with Sweeps

Site: HGTV www.hgtv.com

Membership: No

Contests/Sweeps Section: Yes. Sweepstakes at the very top, or bottom left under More.

Description: HGTV has some great sweepstakes. Well known for the Dream Home Giveaway, HGTV offers a wide selection of contests and sweepstakes. Past sweeps have included the Outdoor Oasis sweepstakes for $25,000 and a trip to Australia, a Coldwell Banker Money Makeover sweep, and a Merry Maids Clean sweepstakes. A lot of info on past sweeps and winners is also included on the site. In addition, sweeps from sister sites as well as various sponsors are available. Our last visit to the HGTV site found the Urban Oasis giveaway promotion valued at over $700,000!

Our Rating: ✪✪✪✪✪

Comments: An outstanding site. The giveaway section is a plus, and just dreaming about winning the million dollar prize package with the dream home is neat, even if the odds are you'll never do it.

Chapter 2 Sites with Sweeps

Site: CMT www.cmt.com

Membership: No

Contests/Sweeps Section: Yes. Sweepstakes tab at bottom, or click on ad.

Description: CMT has some creative sweepstakes. Past sweeps include the Backstage Creations sweep, A Season of Love sweep, a CMT Most Wanted Live prize a day promotion, and a Celebrate Music sweepstakes to name just a few. Prizes from cd's to music players to prize packages have been given away. Our next to last visit found a Party Down South Ultimate Prize Pack giveaway. A trip to NYC to see Kacey Musgraves was featured on our last visit.

Our Rating: ✪✪✪✪✪

Comments: Great site for country music fans, sweeps are a definite plus.

Chapter 2 Sites with Sweeps

Site: Shakefire www.shakefire.com

Membership: No

Contests/Sweeps Section: Yes. Contests tab at top.

Description: The Shakefire site is usually loaded with entertainment info, and contests/sweeps. While the prizes are not huge, there are lots of them. Click the contest tab, and you'll get a page listing books, cd's, dvd's, and video games. Clicking on them will bring up entry pages for giveaways. You won't know the deadline until you click for the second page, though. When we last visited, many of the giveaways were expired. That was disappointing, considering all the prizes being given away on previous visits.

Our Rating: ✪✪1/2

Comments: With so many prizes given away in the past, we'll check back to see if more contests/sweeps are listed in the future.

Chapter 2 Sites with Sweeps

Site: ET Online www.etonline.com

Membership: No

Contests/Sweeps Section: Yes. Bottom left under Browse ET.

Description: On two visits, we were presented with six sweeps, with prizes ranging from movie cd's to a great trip to the People's Choice Awards. The prizes definitely reflect the content of the site. On another visit, we found contests/sweeps for music, electronic equipment, and more. Our next trip found a Cause for Paws giveaway for a celebrity gift bag. No sweepstakes were current when we last visited the site.

Our Rating: ✪✪1/2

Comments: If you're into the celebrity scene, this is your kind of site. Most of the prizes are smaller, but they are unique.

Chapter 2 Sites with Sweeps

Site: Food Network www.foodnetwork.com

Membership: No

Contests/Sweeps Section: Yes. Top or bottom left under More from FN.

Description: Click on Sweepstakes & Contests, and you'll get a page full of contests and sweeps from Food Network and a variety of sister sites. The other sites include DIY and HGTV networks. When we first visited, we found giveaways for a trip to the music city, Nashville, a feature in Food Network magazine, and an appearance on Food Network. Our last visit found a chance to win a trip to NYC to visit the Food Network.

Our Rating: ✪✪✪✪1/2

Comments: The site is reason enough to visit if you love food. The sweeps and contests from Food Network and the sister sites are icing on the cake.

Chapter 2 Sites with Sweeps

Site: Travel Channel www.travelchannel.com

Membership: No

Contests/Sweeps Section: Yes. Sweeps tabs at top and bottom.

Description: Click on the Sweepstakes' tabs, and you'll get sweepstakes, past winners, and current giveaways from sister sites. On our first visit, we didn't find any current sweeps from Travel Channel, but we did find some really good ones featured by sister sites. Those giveaways included an America's Best Cook Challenge, 25 Grand in Your Hand Sweepstakes, and HGTV's Piece of the Dream Sweepstakes. On our next visit we found a Travel Channel Summer Cash Giveaway for $10,000 cash. Our last visit found a $10,000 Ultimate Winter Escape.

Our Rating: ✪✪✪✪1/2

Comments: The Travel Channel site is a great site for anyone who loves to travel. The sweepstakes and contests from Travel Channel and sister sites are just a plus.

Chapter 2 Sites with Sweeps

Site: Golf Channel www.golfchannel.com

Membership: Required for some contests/sweeps.

Contests/Sweeps Section: Yes. Contests tab under About tab at bottom.

Description: On our first visit, we found six contests/sweeps with prizes ranging from equipment to a chance to go behind the scenes at Golf Channel. We found more great giveaways on our next few visits including a chance to win a spot in the Hootie and the Blowfish Pro-Am tournament. Our next visits found even more creative sweeps. Our last visit found a Foursomes Sweepstakes, a Know Your Numbers Sweepstakes, and a chance to win a trip to the 2018 Ryder Cup in Paris.

Our Rating: ✪✪✪1/2

Comments: Some really creative contests/sweeps over the years. We'll check back to see if the giveaways continue to impress.

Chapter 2 Sites with Sweeps

Site: Snackworks www.snackworks.com

Membership: No

Contests/Sweeps Section: Yes. Promotions at top or bottom under Products tab.

Description: Snackworks is now the website for Nabisco products. The former site, NabiscoWorld, always seemed to have a big assortment of contests/sweeps. Past sweeps included prizes such as trips to Hawaii, New York, and San Diego. Other prizes have included a trip to the Baseball Hall of Fame, a MLS soccer camp, and other prizes. One visit found chances to win a summer adventure, a trip to Las Vegas, and the latest in tech gear. On our last visit, we found a chance to win $2,000 and a trip to NYC or LA.

Our Rating: ✪✪1/2

Comments: We'll check back to see if the creative giveaways continue on Snack Works.

Chapter 2 Sites with Sweeps

Site: Woman's Day www.womansday.com

Membership: No

Contests/Sweeps Section: Yes. Click icon at top left, or Giveaways at the bottom of page. You will have to scroll a few times to get to the bottom.

Description: Click on the Giveaways tab, and you'll be presented with a page full of contests/sweeps. Past prizes have ranged from t shirts and floor covering, to trips to Orlando, to concerts. One of our first visits found a host of giveaways, from the Organizing Magic Sweeps to the Walt Disney World Resort Gatherings Sweepstakes. Another visit found 48 sweeps with all sorts of prizes from skincare products to $100,000 to pay bills. Our last visit found even more giveaways! The last count was 69 giveaways of all sizes. Whew!

Our Rating: ✪✪✪✪✪

Comments: Sweepstakes are a big plus on this site that has a little of everything, from info to giveaways.

Chapter 2 Sites with Sweeps

Site: Better Homes & Gardens www.bhg.com

Membership: Yes

Contests/Sweeps Section: No

Description: BHG.com is an information loaded site for home and garden info, and has a variety of contests/sweeps. In our experience, it just depends upon when you visit whether you'll find lots of giveaways or several contests/sweeps. Past contests/sweeps have included a Stock Your Kitchen Cabinets giveaway and an All Star Pet giveaway. Prizes have also included home makeovers worth $25,000 to a $9,000 backyard makeover to an imagination station for a child's room, full of Crayola products. Our last visit, though, found only a daily giveaway for prizes such as a shoe bench and lamp.

Our Rating: ✪✪✪

Comments: We'll check back, but we miss the contests/sweeps section that the site had in the past, and the bigger sweeps that were featured regularly.

Chapter 2 Sites with Sweeps

Site: Family Circle www.familycircle.com

Membership: Yes

Contests/Sweeps Section: Yes. Sweepstakes tab at top under search bar, or bottom under Familycircle.com.

Description: On our first visit the Family Circle site, we found chances to win a dining room makeover, an Orlando family reunion, and more. Our second and third visits found giveaways for a trip to England to a 1 year gym membership. Our most recent visit found seven sweepstakes from Family Circle and associated sites. Prizes ranged from quilting supplies to $6,500 worth of tools.

Our Rating: ✪✪✪✪1/2

Comments: A great variety of sweepstakes from Family Circle, and sites such as Every Day with Rachel Ray and Parent's Magazine.

Chapter 2 Sites with Sweeps

Site: Good Housekeeping www.goodhousekeeping.com

Membership: No

Contests/Sweeps Section: Yes. Click menu icon at top left for the Win tab or click Giveaways tab at bottom.

Description: On our very first visit to the Good Housekeeping site, we found three great sweepstakes; one, a trip to the Cristophe Beverly Hills salon, the second, a twelve day cruise on the Queen Elizabeth II, and the third, a European trip for four people. On our second visit, you could try to win a lunch bag with Tropicana Fruitwise products, a Precor treadmill, free housecleaning for a year, a $25,000 home makeover, or a $25,000 dream vacation. As you can see, quite an assortment of giveaways. Since then, we've found chances to win even more, including a new $50,000 kitchen.

Our Rating: ✪✪✪✪✪

Comments: Love the creative sweepstakes, we'll check back to see if they continue at the same pace.

Chapter 2 Sites with Sweeps

Site: Papercrafts Magazine www.papercraftsmag.com

Membership: No

Contests/Sweeps Section: Yes. Click on Contests tab at top or bottom.

Description: We've visited the Papercrafts' site a number of times, with giveaways featured each time. Although the prizes are not huge, the contests/sweeps go right along with the content of the site, offering winners crafting supplies and packages. The first time we visited, there was only one current contest/ sweep: a December promotion with the chance of winning an assortment of paper products. The last time we visited, we were disappointed when we clicked on the contest tab, an outdated giveaway was all that appeared.

Our Rating: ✪1/2

Comments: The contests/sweeps here are not your bigger prizes, but surely have better odds. We'll check back.

Chapter 2 Sites with Sweeps

Site: Self Magazine www.self.com

Membership: No

Contests/Sweeps Section: No

Description: When we first visited the Self site, there were two sweeps being held; one for a weekend getaway, and one for hair highlighting kits. Our next visit found a chance to win a trip to visit the set of the NBC series, Las Vegas, and a chance to win makeup products. Our third visit found a host of prizes being given away, including makeup, watches, and a trip to the Red Mountain Spa in St. George, Utah. Our next visit found a chance to win a trip to the Breezes Resort. In addition, the Win Prizes! Section had a Previous Winners' list of two years of giveaway winners. No giveaways were featured on our last visit.

Our Rating: ✪✪

Comments: Quite a variety of giveaways from Self Magazine. Too bad the publication is just a women's publication.

Chapter 2 Sites with Sweeps

Site: Outside Info www.outsideinfo.com

Membership: No

Contests/Sweeps Section: Yes. Win It tab at top, or click on ads.

Description: Outside Info had two sweepstakes on its website when we first visited; a chance for a trip to the Australian outback and a chance to win a Yakima rack system. Our second visit found an opportunity to win a guided trip to Mt. Everest from REI Adventures, along with two other giveaways. On our third trip, we found ads for five sweepstakes from various companies. Our fourth visit to the Outside Info site found two giveaways, with one a gear giveaway for one of sixty two prizes. Our last visit produced no new sweepstakes.

Our Rating: ✪✪✪

Comments: We love the variety of contests/sweeps. We'll check back to see what's up next.

Chapter 2 Sites with Sweeps

Site: Redbook www.redbookmag.com

Membership: No

Contests/Sweeps Section: Yes. Click the menu icon to the left, and you will find the Win tab at the bottom.

Description: On our first visit to the old Redbook site, we found chances to win $200 gift certificates, a resort trip, pajamas, and more. On our second visit, we found over $10,000 worth of prizes being given away including a trip to Colorado. Our third and fourth visits found more of the same including prizes such as blenders, grills, cash, and vacations. Our last trip to the site found an assortment of giveaways, including a $1000,000 giveaway. We did notice that the entry period for this sweep extended over a two year period, and no doubt included entries from other Hearst publications.

Our Rating: ✪✪✪✪

Comments: A great variety of giveaways, but entries from these sweeps may be shared among Hearst publications.

Site: F.Y.E. www.fye.com

Membership: No

Contests/Sweeps Section: Win tab about halfway down home page.

Description: Our first visit found six sweeps featuring prizes from FYE gift cards to a guitar signed by Def Leppard to a trip to to Las Vegas. No mention of previous winners listed, but quite an assortment of sweepstakes. The second time we visited, there were sixteen sweeps with prizes from pictures of Butch Walker to trips to Hawaii, the Austin City Limits Music Festival, and Florida. Our next visit found a Guitar of the Week Sweepstakes with fifty two guitars being given away in fifty two weeks. Next time we visited the F.Y.E. site, we found one sweepstakes for a trip to a music festival. On our last visit, we found another giveaway for a music Festival trip and a signed guitar.

Our Rating: ✪✪✪1/2

Comments: A mention of previous winners would be nice, but good assortment of sweepstakes from time to time.

Chapter 2 Sites with Sweeps

Site: People www.people.com

Membership: No

Contests/Sweeps Section: Yes. Bottom of list after clicking menu icon.

Description: When we last visited, the sweepstakes section was running the Stylewatch Giveaways for $4,537 worth of merchandise. When entering, you had the choice of getting a trial issue of People, or entering without one. When we visited again, there were no new sweeps, only a message stating the Stylewatch Giveaways had ended.

Our Rating: ✪

Comments: Our rating is based on just a few visits. The next giveaways could possibly move People's rating upward.

Chapter 2 Sites with Sweeps

Site: Woman's World www.womansworld.com

Membership: No

Contests/Sweeps Section: Yes. Scroll to bottom of page.

Description: Click on the sweepstakes tab, and you'll get Sweepon, a giveaways' production of the Bauer Media Group. When we last visited, there were 10 pages of sweeps with prizes ranging from dvd's to $1,000,000. When entering, you must view a short commercial to process your entry. You will then get a link back to the sweepstakes. The prizes are good, but be prepared for regular e-mails from the Bauer Media Group.

Our Rating: ✪✪✪

Comments: A higher rating would be possible with a few less e-mails.

Chapter 2 Sites with Sweeps

Site: Steamy Kitchen http://steamykitchen.com/

Membership: No

Contests/Sweeps Section: Yes. Top right tab on home page, or bottom.

Description: Steamy Kitchen, a food blog written by Jaden Hair, holds quite a few giveaways throughout the year. In fact, if you click on the link for past winners, you will discover that the blog has given away hundreds of prizes over the last several years. Prizes have ranged from $50 gift cards to cooking merchandise to a Miami food tour. On our first visit, we found two pages of giveaways which included a St. Petersburg Beach stay and an iPad mini. Two pages of giveaways were also featured on our last visit.

Our Rating: ✪✪✪✪

Comments: A surprising number of giveaways from a blog that you may or may not have visited.

Chapter 2 Sites with Sweeps

Site: Leite's Culinaria http://leitesculinaria.com/

Membership: No, but you can sign up for e-mails.

Contests/Sweeps Section: Yes, top row of tabs.

Description: The Leite's Culinaria blog is a surprising, at least for us, place to find lots of giveaways. Granted, most prizes are smaller in nature, but the odds are surely better than the sweepstakes with the blockbuster prizes. When we visited, we found eight pages of giveaways for books, blenders, cookware, cutlery, and more. In addition, the giveaways were really easy to enter, requiring only a name and e-mail address.

Our Rating: ✪✪✪✪

Comments: If you enjoy cooking, you might want to visit the Leite's Culinaria blog for the info and giveaways.

Chapter 3 Sweepstakes/Contests Blogs

Site: Travel Sweepstakes Blogger www.travelsweepstakesblogger.com

Membership: No

Site Design/Navigation: Nice, bright look, sweepstakes take center stage, simple to navigate.

Description: Travel Sweepstakes Blogger is all about what the name Implies; sweepstakes with travel related prizes. On our first visit, we found seventeen sweepstakes with great travel packages as prizes, with trips to LA, Las Vegas, Florida, Switzerland, and Hawaii. Our next visit found nine current sweeps with chances to win trips to the Amazon, London, Canada, Australia, and Paris. Our last visit found even more great trips to places such as Monaco, Las Vegas, Santa Monica, and Hawaii. The only negative is that there are millions that would like to win these trips.

Pros: Nice design, lots of great trips.

Cons: Always more sweepstakes, of course.

Our Rating: ✪✪✪✪

Comments: Just a note about using Travel Sweepstakes Blogger: Click on a headline, you get more info on the sweep; click on link at bottom to go straight to entry page.

Chapter 3 Sweepstakes/Contests Blogs

Site: Sweeties Sweeps www.sweetiessweeps.com

Membership: No, but you can sign up for free e-mail course, and you can also join Sweeties Secret Sweeps($25 yr.) for more local type sweeps.

Site Design/Navigation: At first glance, there's so much info, that the site might seem difficult to navigate, but with a little looking around, it's really not so hard to follow.

Description: The Sweeties Sweeps' website really has a lot of info. You might start with the About page. The page is interesting, as well as motivating. There are also articles about sweeping, and much more. You can look up current sweepstakes by clicking the tabs at top. Whenever we visited, there was an assortment of sweeps, and lots of information. You do have to use the back button to get back to the list of giveaways.

Pros: Lots of info and good sweepstakes.

Cons: Sweeps don't open in a new window.

Our Rating: ✪✪✪✪1/2

Comments: An interesting site for sweepstakes' fans.

Chapter 3 Sweepstakes/Contests Blogs

Site: Enter Online Sweeps http://enteronlinesweeps.com

Membership: No

Site Design/Navigation: Two column blog with current sweeps posted on left side, easy to read.

Description: Along with selected featured sweeps, the home page includes tweets, tags, comments, and categories. Enter Online Sweeps has offered a variety of giveaways from large to small when we visited. Our first visit found prizes from cake decorating kits to a $10,000 trip to Paris. Our last trip found giveaways for jewelry, a $4,000 home makeover, gift cards, and more.

Pros: Variety of sweeps, lots of information.

Cons: Not as many current sweeps as some other sites.

Our Rating: ✪✪✪

Comments: You might not find as many sweeps here, but you might find some really good ones.

Chapter 3 Sweepstakes/Contests Blogs

Site: Ace Contests http://acecontests.com/index.html

Membership: No

Site Design/Navigation: The home page has a personal feel that we like. Click on the USA tab at top for one list of sweeps.

Description: Click on the USA tab at top, and you will get sweepstakes listed by the date posted to the blog. The entry deadline is given after a description of the giveaway. When we visited, there was a good variety of current sweepstakes. Prize categories are listed on the right. You might want to click on the blog tab at top right. We really enjoyed reading some of the posts.

Pros: Good variety of sweeps, relaxing feel of the site.

Cons: Only prize categories available.

Our Rating: ✪✪✪

Comments: We like the personal touch of the site.

Chapter 3 Sweepstakes/Contests Blogs

Site: Only Contests http://onlycontests.com/

Membership: No, but you can sign up for free newsletter.

Site Design/Navigation: Colorful, easy to read blog with tabs at top.

Description: The Only Contests blog is an easy to follow site with lots of information on each giveaway, at first look. While there is not an expiring soon category, the expiration date is prominently displayed at the end of each post. When we last visited, we found a number of great sweeps. In fact, we clicked and clicked the next button, and found at least one hundred current giveaways. Prizes included cash, cars, trips, and much more.

Pros: Lots of great giveaways.

Cons: You must click back button after entering sweepstakes.

Our Rating: ✪✪✪1/2

Comments: On our last visit, Only Contests had more current sweeps than any other blog, that we could remember. Click the second headline beneath the comments tab to go straight to entry page.

Chapter 3 Sweepstakes/Contests Blogs

Site: Lucky Contests www.luckycontests.com

Membership: No, but you can sign up for account which gives you special features, such as the ability to save your favorite sweepstakes.

Site Design/Navigation: Clean, two column design with tabs at top and bottom, latest sweeps featured on home page.

Description: Lucky Contests has gone through a few changes since we first visited the site. The changes have definitely improved the site, however. Latest sweepstakes are featured on the home page, with tabs for prize categories and entry frequency at top. Also included at top are tabs for My Contest feature as well as for a forum. More tabs are located at the bottom including a tab for instant wins. When we last visited, the site had lots of current sweeps, with prizes ranging from trips to St. Lucia, New York, and Killington to gift cards.

Pros: Lots of real good sweepstakes.

Cons: We could have listed a few in the past, but we can't find too many now, unless the number of sweeps decrease in the future.

Our Rating: ✪✪✪✪

Comments: Click on the sweepstakes heading to get info page. Click on the entry button below the sweepstakes to go straight to the sweeps entry page, which opens in new window.

Chapter 3 Sweepstakes/Contests Blogs

Site: Hunt 4 Freebies http://hunt4freebies.com/sweepstakes/

Membership: No

Site Design/Navigation: Large center column with latest sweeps, categories half way down on left, lots of ads.

Description: Probably not a site you would think of when looking for giveaways, but we were pleasantly surprised by the number of up to date sweepstakes. On our last two visits, we clicked through quite a few sweeps before we found any that had expired. The site does have a mixture of smaller and larger sweeps with prizes from cosmetics to blockbuster trips.

Pros: A surprising number of sweepstakes.

Cons: Lots of advertisements.

Our Rating: ✪✪✪

Comments: You won't find a lot of extra information here, but you could find a good giveaway.

Chapter 3 Sweepstakes/Contests Blogs

Site: Sweepstakes Mania www.sweepstakesmania.com

Membership: No

Site Design/Navigation: Easy to read two column blog with latest sweeps featured on home page. Easy to confuse the tabs with some of the ads, though.

Description: On our last visit, we found some good sweepstakes with prizes ranging from gift cards to Disney vacations. Latest sweeps are featured on home page with categories at both the top and the bottom of the page. Some of the ads look very similar to the real Sweepstakes Mania tabs. There is a tab at top for Still Active Sweeps which might be a good idea for sweeps presented in a blog. Also, there is a box for comments at bottom right.

Pros: Wide variety of good sweeps.

Cons: When you click on a sweep, you get info page instead of going straight to the sweep, although some might like this feature.

Our Rating: ✪✪✪1/2

Comments: Lots of good sweeps, but also lots of ads.

Chapter 3 Sweepstakes/Contests Blogs

Site: Sweepstakes Fanatics www.sweepstakesfanatics.com

Membership: No, but you can subscribe to free newsletter.

Site Design/Navigation: Easy to follow two column blog. There are some ads that could be confused with the blog's sweeps' categories.

Description: Sweepstakes Fanatics, like some other blogs, has a two step process to enter sweepstakes. Click on the sweepstakes' title or the More Info tab to get more info on the sweep, and the enter sweepstakes link. The site does provide some good info on the giveaways, but does not list the deadline on the first page. The first time we visited, there were sweeps for trips to New York, Hawaii, and Las Vegas. In addition, there were sweeps for the HGTV dream home, cruises, and more.

Pros: Some great sweeps, easy to read blog.

Cons: No deadline on first page, however, there is a tab at top for sweeps sorted by expiration date.

Our Rating: ✪✪✪✪

Comments: You'll find tabs for categories at the top, bottom, and right side of home page. You will also find listings of newest sweepstakes and popular sweeps on the right.

Chapter 3 Sweepstakes/Contests Blogs

Site: Contest Bee www.contestbee.com

Membership: No

Site Design/Navigation: Basic two column blog with prize categories on right side, latest sweeps in center.

Description: Contest Bee is an easy to read blog with latest sweepstakes featured by listing date. There are prize categories on right, along with tabs for instant wins and daily entry. On our first visit, we found some good sweeps with prizes ranging from a Paris trip to an Airstream trailer to beauty products. The sweeps open in a new window, which is always nice. On our last visit, we found sweepstakes with more great prizes, including trips to England, Florida, and British Columbia.

Pros: Some good sweeps, and they open in a new window.

Cons: Banner ad takes away from look.

Our Rating: ✪✪✪✪

Comments: Easy to navigate blog with some good sweeps.

Chapter 3 Sweepstakes/Contests Blogs

Site: Sweepstakes Mag www.sweepstakesmag.com

Membership: No, but you can subscribe to updates.

Site Design/Navigation: Sweepstakes Mag has at least five sections on the home page, including latest sweeps, must-see, trending, and featured. Tabs are located at the top, bottom, and right side.

Description: When you click on a sweepstakes listed on the Sweepstakes Mag blog, you'll get a page with more information on the selected sweep. The link to enter the giveaway can be found under Details. After you enter the sweepstakes, you will have to click to return to the sweeps list to enter others. The site does offer some good sweeps from companies such as Coke, Marriott, and Travel Channel.

Pros: Lots of info on sweeps.

Cons: Two-step process to enter sweeps.

Our Rating: ✪✪✪

Comments: Some good sweeps here.

Chapter 4 Instant Win

Chapter 4 Instant Win

Site: Snazzy Win http://snazzywin.com/

Membership: No, but an e-mail address gets you daily updates.

Site Design/Navigation: Lots of info and color on home page, tabs at top, easy navigation.

Description: If you notice, by the tabs at top, the site has more than instant wins. In fact, Snazzy Wins has sweepstakes as well as instant wins . The home page features free stuff, coupons, instant wins, and sweepstakes. When we first visited, we found quite a few sweeps and instant wins. Some of the featured listings had both grand prizes and smaller instant win prizes. However, when we last visited, we found lots of expired listings. We hope that this is only a temporary thing, since we like the site.

Pros: Good number of instant wins and sweeps, lots of info.

Cons: Lots of expired instant wins and sweeps on our last visit.

Our Rating: ✪✪

Comments: We'll check back to see if there are updates.

Chapter 4 Instant Win

Site: Our Instant Win www.ourinstantwin.com

Membership: No

Site Design/Navigation: Very simple one column list of instant wins, with no ads.

Description: At first glance, Our Instant Win may not give you the impression that there will be much to see. However, after scrolling down the page, you'll see just how many instant wins are posted. While there are not any categories on the top, bottom, or side, the posts are divided into sections. The sections include multiple daily entries, daily entry, special circumstances, and more.

Pros: Lots of instant wins, no ads.

Cons: Instant wins not listed by expiration dates.

Our Rating: ✪✪✪✪

Comments: We can't believe that the site can have this many instant wins with no advertisements.

Chapter 4 Instant Win

Site: Freebie Shark www.freebieshark.com

Membership: No

Site Design/Navigation: Click Instant Win Games & Sweeps on the right to access the instant wins. You will get a list of instant wins, followed by sweeps.

Description: Freebie Shark might not sound like a place to find many instant win games. Check the site out, and you might be surprised. A click on the instant wins tab at right takes you to a one column list of instant wins and sweeps. When we last visited, we found over sixty current instant win listings, and the games were listed by expiration date, which was nice.

Pros: Lots of current instant wins.

Cons: Not too much info on list of games. (Then again, you might like the idea of only the prizes, entry, and deadline.)

Our Rating: ✪✪✪1/2

Comments: Lots of games listed on this surprising site.

Chapter 4 Instant Win

Site: Instant Win Crazy www.instantwincrazy.com

Membership: No

Site Design/Navigation: Big type, three column design with tabs at top, tags at right, and more categories at bottom.

Description: Instant Win Crazy has been redesigned since our first visit to the site. We really liked the easy to follow former design. We're not sure if the new design is better, but that is just our opinion. We do know that there were not as many instant wins listed on our last visits. At the top of the home page, you will find plenty of tabs, from instant wins to spin to win to winning tips and hints.

Pros: Lots of info and categories, games open in new window.

Cons: Not as many listings as before.

Our Rating: ✪✪✪1/2

Comments: We'll visit again to see the number of listed games.

Chapter 5 Online Games

Chapter 5 Online Games

Site: Gamesville www.gamesville.com

Membership: Yes

Site Design/Navigation: Colorful site, main tabs at top, easy to follow.

Description: Gamesville is a site that has been around for a while. Years ago, it offered huge prizes. These days, the prizes are much smaller, with daily, weekly, and monthly drawings for $25, $100, and $500. While the games are well done, they are limited in number compared to other game sites. When we last visited, there were eleven games including several bingo games, solitaire, and such games as Fruit Frenzy and Frantic Fish. Play is required to earn entries to sweepstakes.

Pros: Colorful graphics, free play, fun games.

Cons: Limited number of games, no prizes larger than $500.

Our Rating: ✪✪✪1/2

Comments: Nice site especially for fans of bingo type games.

Chapter 5 Online Games

Site: Pogo www.pogo.com

Membership: Yes. Paid membership offers more games and prizes.

Site Design/Navigation: Lots of games and info on home page, but easy to navigate when you get familiar with site.

Description: Pogo offers a large assortment of games in categories such as puzzle, card, board, word, hidden object, and more. Such well known games such as Wheel of Fortune and Family Feud are included. Players can earn entries to three daily drawings of $25 and $50. Some games are quite addictive, and you might get hooked.

Pros: Nice assortment of fun games.

Cons: No real huge prizes.

Our Rating: ✪✪✪✪

Comments: Nice site with some really addictive games.

Chapter 5 Online Games

Site: HSN www.hsn.com

Membership: Yes

Site Design/Navigation: Arcade tab at top takes you to page with featured games, game tabs, and reward store tabs, easy to follow directions.

Description: The HSN games section offered thirty seven games when we last visited the site. Games are varied, with easy to figure out instructions, challenging, and fun to play. Players play games, and earn tickets, which can be entered into drawings for prizes. There were four pages of prizes when we last visited, with prizes ranging from cosmetics to luggage to designer bags. Prize pages list the number of tickets that are required to enter drawings, and the number of days left until prize giveaways.

Pros: Fun games, easy to enter giveaways.

Cons: No huge prizes.

Our Rating: ✪✪✪✪1/2

Comments: Drawings for prizes a plus on this site.

Chapter 5 Online Games

Site: Slingo www.slingo.com

Membership: Yes

Site Design/Navigation: Featured games displayed on home page, with tabs for a variety of categories at top.

Site Design/Navigation: Slingo offers a variety of games including bingo, casino, card, puzzle, and trivia and word games. Players play games to earn coins for entries into sweepstakes.

Pros: Some good games.

Cons: Intermission between games.

Our Rating: ✪✪✪

Comments: Fun game site where you can earn coins for entries into sweeps. The only problem is that there are lots of entries.

Chapter 5 Online Games

Site: Game Show Network www.gsn.com

Membership: Yes

Site Design/Navigation: Lots of info on home page. It may take a while to to get familiar with site.

Description: GSN's site offers free games along with paid cash games. At first, it might be a little confusing. For free play, players earn oodles for playing games. These oodles can then be used to enter sweepstakes for cash prizes, gift cards, and discounts. Recent prizes have included $250, Starbucks' gift cards, and an electronics' charger. Games offered include word games, strategy, and arcade games, as well as games such as Family Feud, The Price is Right, and Wheel of Fortune. You'll need to look over the full games' list to distinguish between free and paid games.

Pros: Lots of games including well known television games.

Cons: The amount of time to look at ads, learning the difference between tokens, oodles, and cash games.

Our Rating: ✪✪✪1/2

Comments: Prepare for a little time to navigate around the site at first.

Chapter 5 Online Games

Site: Daily Break www.dailybreak.com

Membership: Yes

Site Design/Navigation: Very easy to navigate once you find your way around the site.

Description: On the Daily Break site, you take quizzes and polls to earn coins. You can then redeem these coins to enter drawings for prizes such as gift cards and merchandise. You can also redeem your coins for discounts from selected merchants. In, addition, you can spin a prize wheel each day for prizes or more coins.

Pros: Easy to take quizzes and polls, ease of navigation

Cons: No really big prizes.

Our Rating: ✪✪✪✪

Comments: Some might say that the polls can be silly, but they are not to be taken very seriously. The site is all in good fun, with a chance to win prizes.

Index

Other Sites

Notes

Passwords A

Passwords B

Passwords C

Passwords D

Passwords E

Passwords # F

Passwords H

Passwords # I

Passwords J

Passwords K

Passwords L

Passwords N

Passwords **O**

Passwords # P

Passwords Q

Passwords # R

Passwords **S**

Passwords T

Passwords U

Passwords V

Passwords W

Passwords X

Passwords Y

Passwords # Z

www.ingramcontent.com/pod-product-compliance
Lightning Source LLC
Chambersburg PA
CBHW070811280326
41934CB00012B/3146

* 9 7 8 0 6 1 5 9 6 9 3 0 5 *